The Dreams and Thoughts of one man

Written by: Reyes j Charnin

The dream of many dreams

Caressing your body in my dreams.

Thinking of you with every thought that runs through my head.
As i ask myself was it worth it all ?

As i sink in the Quicksand called love i think of the memories we made.

Reminiscing on how beautiful your smile was and how it gave me life.
Loving you paid a price and damaged my happiness.

Oh how careless you became to those who attached themselves to you.

This feeling is so powerful it can tear someone in half and stitch them back together again.

Caressing your body in my dreams.

The dream of many dreams

"Beauty is the key"
Not only on the outside but the inside also contains,
for beauty can be mistaken for a much stronger power.
Everyone holds beauty whether it's in their looks, heart, poetry, Art,
Etc...

The dream of many dreams

As i sit still i keep

Thinking of you and

how happy you make me and the feeling

That appears when i see you is astonishing.

The dream of many dreams

Having an open heart can be tough,
Being able to show your true self to someone is the hardest thing
Being able to trust them is the most difficult.
If someone opened up to you, you mean something to that one person.
Just Wishing you were a happier person when i met you

The dream of many dreams

A Fairytale romance can only exist
In the most fake movies and fictional books
If being in a fairytale with you was a choice
We'd be happier.

The dream of many dreams

The Garden was full of flowers and you picked the most prettiest
Leaving the others to die...why?
Now that my tears have watered the garden, Its seems to be eye catching to you again.
Is growth too much for you to handle?
It was forbidden for you to enter my Garden
Yet you still wander around it
GOODBYE!!!

The dream of many dreams

A king once lived

After giving his all to you, you gave up
He tried his best to keep you and you left him.
Leaving him will make him wither away so you thought.
Sorrow was upon him, after he grew stronger and realized you weren't worthy of his love you came crawling back begging
And this time he didn't give up his throne or heart.
He said, "Now you know what type of sorrow and pain i felt, BE Gone!"

The dream of many dreams

Designated to be the one but you didn't have the correct directions, Designated to be the one yet you second guessed if you were in love, Designated to hurt him but you've failed because we've all been down this road before.

The dream of many dreams

Can Being Pure Exist?

Only in the most insane lover

Can loyalty Exist?

Only in the most unsure and self judging people

Can happiness exist?

Only in the most Growth mindset

Being happy, loyal, and pure only lay in the most strongest people

The dream of many dreams

Never again will i play that game
I said this once and still let it happen.
Leading down hill it was, but i regained my self, stood strong
And fought my battles.

The dream of many dreams

Needing can change your
Perspective on something even tho that need never
Exceeded to its best potential
Yet you still strive for it.

The dream of many dreams

Writing your name on my heart was the easiest thing
But taking it off is a challenge
Change is something that i will be going through soon
Don't be scared i warned you.

The dream of many dreams

An Addict sticks to its usage,
They will always have their relapses, there will
always be that thing that will hold them back.
Trying to recover is hard and so is loving something,
Tearing me to pieces is what love does
Now we just need to help put each other back together again.

The dream of many dreams

Individually you are different, no one can be compared to you
You are unique in your own way.
You handle things differently an especially when it is urgent
You are the key to my happiness.

The dream of many dreams

Wine is a mysterious thing
When drinking wine i forget the feeling of emptiness in my heart
I forget how it felt to love
But i'm in a daze that will soon break
wine is a mysterious thing.

The dream of many dreams

Text me

Call me

Talk to me

I am Here.

The dream of many dreams

You were 2nd to him

But the first to enter my mind

The dream of many dreams

For love once was a beautiful thing
Then, you neglected my heart
Broke me into pieces and left me to wither away

The dream of many dreams

Sneaking a cookie out of the jar
is the way you were when you took
my heart from my chest

The dream of many dreams

When i was a child i always
Knew to get back up after
Getting hurt but what do i
do now after being heart broken?

The dream of many dreams

When it comes to love
Will i have to poison my heart
in order to love you?

The dream of many dreams

You have to love the lonely
Cherish the moments you had
And move on.

The dream of many dreams

*After **wandering** through the maze of Love you'll ask yourself if it could've been better,*
After the maze growth will take place in life and nothing can get in the way, unless you let it.
*As soon as you know it you'll be back **by his side** because you gave him your all, as soon as you know it you'll be alone **again.***

Boys and Girls:

The dream of many dreams

Boys and Girls are in separate worlds

They live in their universe

I am viewed as helpful

Im expected to learn from my mistakes

Because i'm a boy in my family i feel like an outcast

Someday i want to live a normal life and have normal kids

Until then i am a piece of stone that will sit in the same place

forever until i get moved

The dream of many dreams

Father,
Someone i could rely on when i needed him the most,
Someone who has taught me a lot in such a short time,
Someone who was taken from me at such a young age.

Dear Father,
I just want to say thank you. As i grow to the man that i desire i will use the knowledge you fed to me as a young boy, i will never forget you. Even though you cannot physically be here i will always love you and cherish the moments we had together.

The dream of many dreams

Just write out what's wrong,

Fix yourself,

You probably don't know what your doing,

But don't ask for help because they'll make it worse

Just learn,

Fix yourself.

The dream of many dreams

As the butterfly flew across the young man's face he realized how slow things could be in life. He realized that it takes time to grow out of your cocoon and learn how to fly. He realized that growth will take time, that nothing will come fast in the story of love.

The dream of many dreams

Why?

You and your selfish ways have conquered many things except me.

Why?

As i repeat the voice messages you left me of your "sincere apologies" yet you still act the same.

Why?

As i ask myself after letting you back in my life.

The dream of many dreams

I Dream about what i think about during the day, i realize that i overthink some situations and jump to conclusions alot. I Try not to think of it too much but it just stays there and creeps up on me…

The dream of many dreams

Perfection is what you Visualize when you first laid your eyes on him.
To him deep down inside nothing was perfect and will never be.
(until you meet each other.)

The dream of many dreams

You believed in him, he set the timer.
He left before you could fully express yourself to him,
Ashamed he felt after leaving you,
He exploded into tears, you laughed just as he did to you.

The dream of many dreams

A dream you thought it was but it wasn't...
Forever was the thought running through your head at the time
Right?
Loneliness was the key i guess.

The dream of many dreams

Being able to see people grow out of their shells is amazing
And change can motivate you to do the same thing.

The dream of many dreams

As you robbed me of the love that
i had for you, taking every ounce of it
leaving me to doubt what "love" is.

The dream of many dreams

Will i have to play the victim in this crazy love story again?
Sooner or later you'll be the one paying the price that you weighed on my precious heart.

The dream of many dreams

Sending me messages wont fix it
blowing up my phone will get you blocked
You showed me who you truly are
Now leave me alone

The dream of many dreams

Forever doesn't last these days even if u put in your all to someone who would care, again sorry to say but forever doesn't last these days.

The dream of many dreams

My hair, My skin, my thoughts, the fear running through my veins, your on my mind while in with him. Why? Please leave me ALONE now's the time to cleanse and run away.

The dream of many dreams

Fries Dipped in ranch> wings dipped in ranch> chicken stripes dipped in ranch> me dipped in ranch. Everything dipped in ranch. :)

The dream of many dreams

You've loved him, he hurt you. You'd go back to him with every bit of your heart and he still kept hiding shit from you. Of course you loved him for who he was but not how he treated you and your heart. As you search for the boy you first met you'll find the man he'll become.

The dream of many dreams

My love is stronger than your pride. All i remember was the sweet love that you gave as they say love is the greatest weapon to use in the war called love.

The dream of many dreams

Why chase after someone who doesn't want you?
Just be with the one who will give you their all.

The dream of many dreams

Love is so powerful it can make you the saddest bitch and happiest bitch out there at the same time. :/

The dream of many dreams

As i stand in front of your headstone i think of how beautiful your smile was. As i'm reminiscing on the long summer nights hanging out on the swings. As your body lays to rest your soul will flow freely to the gates of heaven. Forever in my heart and on my mind i love you D.A.A <3

The dream of many dreams

As time speeds up where did my love for you go?
Why did i stop loving you?
Why did you stop loving me?
Why didn't we go on with life?

Oh right you cheated...

The dream of many dreams

I have every reason why i should move on but i let you come back into my life, i let you trap my heart in the cage made of lust.
Your the reason why i am who i am today.

The dream of many dreams

Everything about you

Your eyes,

Your smile,

Your soul,

Was so precious but your heart was stone cold.

The dream of many dreams

Your not okay, you were never okay.

The dream of many dreams

Don't go try to fix someone else when your breaking apart yourself.

The dream of many dreams

You were the highlight of my life. You made me love unconditionally and gave me butterflies in my stomach when we were around each other. YOU helped me through the thick and thin. On my toughest days you were by my side, But you walked away from me. You walked away as if we never met, never made eye contact, never kissed, never touched. I still love you…

The dream of many dreams

S uppourt my decisions

U nderstand me

C ommit to our love

K eep me

M ake me proud

Y ours forever

D ance the night away

I dealistict

C oncealment

K eep to yourself

I loved you now, now your a normal person in the world with no care in your heart.

www.ingramcontent.com/pod-product-compliance
Lightning Source LLC
Chambersburg PA
CBHW021957060426
42444CB00042B/809